LIMITED LOAN
106072

Camden County Library
8 ECHELON MALL
VOORHEES, N. J. 08043

D1789622

j821.008 Ada
Adams, Adrienne
Poetry of earth

C 106072

Camden County Free Library
8 Echelon Mall
Voorhees, N. J. 08043

POETRY OF EARTH

POETRY OF EARTH

Selected and illustrated by **Adrienne Adams**

Published by Charles Scribner's Sons • New York

To Mandy Hotchkiss

Copyright © 1972 Adrienne Adams Anderson

This book published simultaneously in the United States of America and in Canada. Copyright under the Berne Convention. All rights reserved. No part of this book may be reproduced in any form without the permission of Charles Scribner's Sons.

A-8.72[RZ]

Printed in the United States of America.
Library of Congress Catalog Card Number 70-39577
SBN 684-13012-2 (cloth, RB)

ACKNOWLEDGMENTS

"The Sandhill Crane" by Mary Austin: From *Children Sing in the Far West*. Reprinted by permission of Houghton Mifflin Company, publishers.

"Zebra" by Isak Dinesen: From *Out of Africa*, by Isak Dinesen. Copyright 1937 and renewed 1965 by Rungstedlundfonden. Reprinted by permission of Random House, Inc.

"Dust of Snow," "Stopping by Woods on a Snowy Evening," and a portion of "A Considerable Speck" by Robert Frost: From *The Poetry of Robert Frost*, edited by Edward Connery Lathem. Copyright 1923, © 1969 by Holt, Rinehart and Winston, Inc. Copyright 1942, 1951 by Robert Frost. Copyright © 1970 by Lesley Frost Ballantine. Reprinted by permission of Holt, Rinehart and Winston, Inc.

"The Prayer of the Little Ducks" by Carmen Bernos de Gasztold: From *Prayers from the Ark*, by Carmen Bernos de Gasztold, translated by Rumer Godden. Copyright © 1962 by Rumer Godden. Reprinted by permission of The Viking Press Inc. and Macmillan London & Basingstoke.

"Nursery Snail" by Ruth Herschberger: Reprinted by permission of the author.

"Prayer for Reptiles" by Patricia Hubbell: Copyright © 1965 by Patricia Hubbell. From *8 A.M. Shadows*. Used by permission of Atheneum Publishers.

"Bats" and "The Bird of Night" by Randall Jarrell: Reprinted with permission of The Macmillan Company from *The Bat-Poet* by Randall Jarrell. Copyright © by The Macmillan Company, 1963, 1964.

"The Wild Geese Returning" by Tsumori Kunimoto: From *Japanese Poetry: The "Uta"*, by Arthur Waley. Reprinted by permission of Alison Waley.

"The Ballad of Red Fox" by Melvin Walker La Follette: From *The Clever Body* by Melvin Walker La Follette. First published in *The New Yorker*. Reprinted by permission of the author.

"Crows" and "Tiger Lily" by David McCord: From *Far and Few* by David McCord. Reprinted by permission of Little, Brown and Company, publishers. Copyright 1934, 1952, by David McCord.

"The Buck in the Snow" by Edna St. Vincent Millay: From *Collected Poems*, Harper & Row, Copyright 1928, 1955 by Edna St. Vincent Millay and Norma Millay Ellis.

"Here She Is" by Mary Britton Miller: Reprinted by permission of the author.

"Overheard on a Saltmarsh" by Harold Monro: From *Collected Poems* by Harold Monro. Reprinted by permission of Gerald Duckworth & Co. Ltd., publishers.

"The Meadow Mouse" by Theodore Roethke: Copyright © 1963 by Beatrice Roethke, Administratrix of the Estate of Theodore Roethke from *Collected Poems of Theodore Roethke*. Reprinted by permission of Doubleday & Company, Inc.

"Buffalo Dusk" and "Summer Stars" by Carl Sandburg: From *Smoke and Steel* by Carl Sandburg, copyright, 1920, by Harcourt Brace Jovanovich, Inc.; copyright, 1948, by Carl Sandburg. Reprinted by permission of the publisher.

"Measure Me, Sky" by Leonora Speyer: From *Slow Wall: Poems*, by Leonora Speyer. Copyright 1939, 1946, 1951 and renewed 1967 by the Estate of Leonora Speyer. Reprinted by permission of Alfred A. Knopf, Inc.

"The Goat Paths," "Little Things," and "The Snare" by James Stephens: Reprinted with permission of The Macmillan Company from *Collected Poems* by James Stephens. Copyright 1915, 1926 by The Macmillan Company, renewed 1943 by James Stephens, 1954 by Cynthia Stephens; also by permission of Mrs. Iris Wise, Macmillan London & Basingstoke, and The Macmillan Company of Canada Limited.

"Living Tenderly" by May Swenson: Reprinted by permission of Charles Scribner's Sons from *To Mix with Time* by May Swenson. Copyright © 1963 May Swenson.

"The Sea Turtle and the Shark" by Melvin B. Tolson: From *Muse of Fire*, edited by H. Edward Richardson and Frederick B. Shroyer. Copyright 1965 by Twayne Publishers, Inc. Reprinted by permission of the publishers.

"Egrets" by Judith Wright: From *Collected Poems 1942–1970* by Judith Wright. Reprinted by permission of the author and Angus & Robertson Ltd., Publishers.

"Velvet Shoes" by Elinor Wylie: Copyright 1921 and renewed 1929 by William Rose Benet. Reprinted from *Collected Poems of Elinor Wylie*, by Elinor Wylie, by permission of Alfred A. Knopf, Inc.

"To a Squirrel at Kyle-na-no" by William Butler Yeats. Reprinted with permission of The Macmillan Company from *Collected Poems* by William Butler Yeats. Copyright 1919 by The Macmillan Company, renewed 1947 by Bertha Georgie Yeats; also by permission of Mr. M. B. Yeats and The Macmillan Company of Canada Limited.

"Look, the Sea!" by William Zorach: From *Poetry*, Vol. XII, September 1918. Copyright 1918 by The Modern Poetry Association. Reprinted by permission of the Editor of *Poetry*.

Poetry of Earth

9 LIVING TENDERLY by May Swenson
10 BATS by Randall Jarrell
12 LOOK, THE SEA! by William Zorach
13 WHITE BUTTERFLIES by Algernon Charles Swinburne
14 BUFFALO DUSK by Carl Sandburg
16 SUMMER STARS by Carl Sandburg
17 OVERHEARD ON A SALTMARSH by Harold Monro
18 CROWS by David McCord
19 DUST OF SNOW by Robert Frost
20 A NARROW FELLOW IN THE GRASS by Emily Dickinson
21 TIGER LILY by David McCord
22 THE SNARE by James Stephens
23 A CONSIDERABLE SPECK by Robert Frost
24 THE MEADOW MOUSE by Theodore Roethke

Page	Title
25	NURSERY SNAIL by Ruth Herschberger
26	THE EAGLE by Alfred, Lord Tennyson
28	TO A SQUIRREL AT KYLE-NA-NO by William Butler Yeats
29	THE BUCK IN THE SNOW by Edna St. Vincent Millay
30	THE GOAT PATHS by James Stephens
32	THE BIRD OF NIGHT by Randall Jarrell
34	HERE SHE IS by Mary Britton Miller
35	ZEBRA by Isak Dinesen
36	STOPPING BY WOODS ON A SNOWY EVENING by Robert Frost
37	VELVET SHOES by Elinor Wylie
38	THE PRAYER OF THE LITTLE DUCKS by Carmen Bernos de Gasztold
39	THE SANDHILL CRANE by Mary Austin
40	THE SEA TURTLE AND THE SHARK by Melvin B. Tolson
42	PRAYER FOR REPTILES by Patricia Hubbell
43	THE BALLAD OF RED FOX by Melvin Walker La Follette
45	EGRETS by Judith Wright
46	MEASURE ME, SKY by Leonora Speyer
47	LITTLE THINGS by James Stephens
48	THE WILD GEESE RETURNING by Tsumori Kunimoto

Living Tenderly

May Swenson

My body a rounded stone
with a pattern of smooth seams.
My head a short snake,
retractive, projective.
My legs come out of their sleeves
or shrink within,
and so does my chin.
My eyelids are quick clamps.

My back is my roof.
I am always at home.
I travel where my house walks.
It is a smooth stone.
It floats within the lake,
or rests in the dust.
My flesh lives tenderly
inside its bone.

Bats
Randall Jarrell

A bat is born
Naked and blind and pale.
His mother makes a pocket of her tail
And catches him. He clings to her long fur
By his thumbs and toes and teeth.
And then the mother dances through the night
Doubling and looping, soaring, somersaulting—
Her baby hangs on underneath.
All night, in happiness, she hunts and flies.
Her high sharp cries
Like shining needlepoints of sound
Go out into the night and, echoing back,
Tell her what they have touched.
She hears how far it is, how big it is,
Which way it's going:
She lives by hearing.
The mother eats the moths and gnats she catches
In full flight; in full flight
The mother drinks the water of the pond
She skims across. Her baby hangs on tight.
Her baby drinks the milk she makes him
In moonlight or starlight, in mid-air.
Their single shadow, printed on the moon
Or fluttering across the stars,
Whirls on all night; at daybreak
The tired mother flaps home to her rafter.
The others all are there.
They hang themselves up by their toes,
They wrap themselves in their brown wings.

Bunched upside-down, they sleep in air.
Their sharp ears, their sharp teeth, their quick sharp faces
Are dull and slow and mild.
All the bright day, as the mother sleeps,
She folds her wings about her sleeping child.

Look, the Sea!

William Zorach

Look, the sea—how it lifts me in its arms like a child!
Oh, how I love to ride on the white foam of the waves
And dive down into the deep bottom of the sea!

Look, the sun—how it burns me like a leaf!
Oh, how I love to bathe in the hot rays of the sun
And burn like a flame in the sands!

Look, the moon—how it rides me in sky!
Oh, how I love to sail on the shining edge of the clouds,
And sleep in the cool depths of the blue!

White Butterflies

Algernon Charles Swinburne

Fly, white butterflies, out to sea,
Frail, pale wings for the wind to try,
Small white wings that we scarce can see,
    Fly!

Some fly light as a laugh of glee,
Some fly soft as a long, low sigh;
All to the haven where each would be,
    Fly!

Buffalo Dusk

Carl Sandburg

The buffaloes are gone.
And those who saw the buffaloes are gone.
Those who saw the buffaloes by thousands and
    how they pawed the prairie sod into dust
    with their hoofs, their great heads down
    pawing on in a great pageant of dusk,
Those who saw the buffaloes are gone.
And the buffaloes are gone.

Summer Stars
Carl Sandburg

Bend low again, night of summer stars.
So near you are, sky of summer stars,
So near, a long arm man can pick off stars,
Pick off what he wants in the sky bowl,
So near you are, summer stars,
So near, strumming, strumming,
So lazy and hum-strumming.

Overheard on a Saltmarsh

Harold Monro

Nymph, nymph, what are your beads?

Green glass, goblin. Why do you stare at them?

Give them me.

No.

Give them me. Give them me.

No.

Then I will howl all night in the reeds,
Lie in the mud and howl for them.

Goblin, why do you love them so?

They are better than stars or water,
Better than voices of winds that sing,
Better than any man's fair daughter,
Your green glass beads on a silver ring.

Hush, I stole them out of the moon.

Give me your beads, I want them.

No.

I will howl in a deep lagoon
For your green glass beads, I love them so.
Give them me. Give them me.

No.

Crows
David McCord

I like to walk
And hear the black crows talk.

I like to lie
And watch crows sail the sky.

I like the crow
That wants the wind to blow:

I like the one
That thinks the wind is fun.

I like to see
Crows spilling from a tree,

And try to find
The top crow left behind.

I like to hear
Crows caw that spring is near.

I like the great
Wild clamor of crow hate

Three farms away
When owls are out by day.

I like the slow
Tired homeward-flying crow;

I like the sight
Of crows for my good night.

Dust of Snow

Robert Frost

The way a crow
Shook down on me
The dust of snow
From a hemlock tree

Has given my heart
A change of mood
And saved some part
Of a day I had rued.

A Narrow Fellow in the Grass
Emily Dickinson

A narrow fellow in the grass
Occasionally rides;
You may have met him,—did you not?
His notice sudden is.

The grass divides as with a comb,
A spotted shaft is seen;
And then it closes at your feet
And opens further on.

He likes a boggy acre,
A floor too cool for corn.
Yet when a child, and barefoot,
I more than once, at morn,

Have passed, I thought, a whip-lash
Unbraiding in the sun,—
When, stooping to secure it,
It wrinkled, and was gone.

Several of nature's people
I know, and they know me;
I feel for them a transport
Of cordiality;

But never met this fellow,
Attended or alone,
Without a tighter breathing,
And zero at the bone.

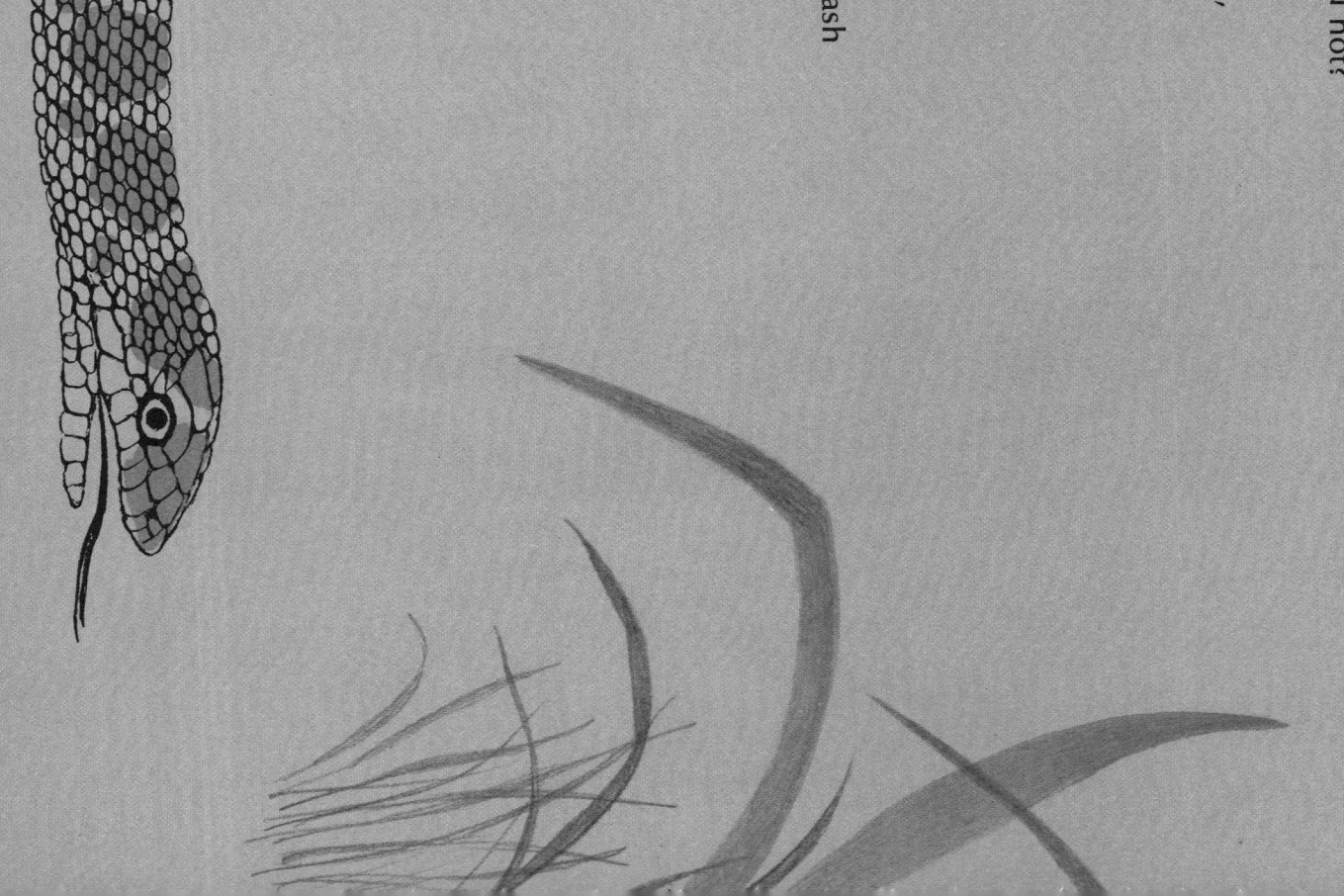

Tiger Lily

David McCord

The tiger lily is a panther,
Orange to black spot:
Her tongue is the velvet pretty anther,
And she's in the vacant lot.

The cool day lilies grow beside her,
But they are done now and dead,
And between them a little silver spider
Hangs from a thread.

The Snare
James Stephens

I hear a sudden cry of pain!
There is a rabbit in a snare:
Now I hear the cry again,
But I cannot tell from where.

But I cannot tell from where
He is calling out for aid;
Crying on the frightened air,
Making everything afraid,

Making everything afraid
Wrinkling up his little face,
As he cries again for aid;
And I cannot find the place!

And I cannot find the place
Where his paw is in the snare;
Little one! Oh, little one!
I am searching everywhere.

A Considerable Speck (Microscopic)

Robert Frost

A speck that would have been beneath my sight
On any but a paper sheet so white
Set off across what I had written there.
And I had idly poised my pen in air
To stop it with a period of ink,
When something strange about it made me think.
This was no dust speck by my breathing blown,
But unmistakably a living mite
With inclinations it could call its own.
It paused as with suspicion of my pen,
And then came racing wildly on again
To where my manuscript was not yet dry;
Then paused again and either drank or smelt—
With loathing, for again it turned to fly.
Plainly with an intelligence I dealt.
It seemed too tiny to have room for feet,
Yet must have had a set of them complete
To express how much it didn't want to die.
It ran with terror and with cunning crept.
It faltered: I could see it hesitate;
Then in the middle of the open sheet
Cower down in desperation to accept
Whatever I accorded it of fate.

. . . . .

Since it was nothing I knew evil of
I let it lie there till I hope it slept.

I have a mind myself and recognize
Mind when I meet with it in any guise.
No one can know how glad I am to find
On any sheet the least display of mind.

The Meadow Mouse

Theodore Roethke

1. In a shoe box stuffed in an old nylon stocking
Sleeps the baby mouse I found in the meadow,
Where he trembled and shook beneath a stick
Till I caught him up by the tail and brought him in,
Cradled in my hand,
A little quaker, the whole body of him trembling,
His absurd whiskers sticking out like a cartoon-mouse,
His feet like small leaves,
Little lizard-feet,
Whitish and spread wide when he tried to struggle away,
Wriggling like a miniscule puppy.

   Now he's eaten his three kinds of cheese and drunk
      from his bottle-cap watering-trough—
So much he just lies in one corner,
His tail curled under him, his belly big
As his head; his bat-like ears
Twitching, tilting toward the least sound.

   Do I imagine he no longer trembles
When I come close to him?
He seems no longer to tremble.

2. But this morning the shoe-box house on the back porch
      is empty.
Where has he gone, my meadow mouse,
My thumb of a child that nuzzled in my palm?—
To run under the hawk's wing,
Under the eye of the great owl watching from the elm-tree,
To live by courtesy of the shrike, the snake, the tom-cat.

Nursery Snail
Ruth Herschberger

The garden snail,
moist in its bed,
arises,
tickled by the grass
at its feet
and the new dew.

Its horns steal out
for comfort,
finding
moss at the touch
and the new dew.

Snail-paced,
the garden snail
ventures
a shell's length,
and finding you,
withdraws,
snag-toothed,
smoulder-still,
from the sweet grass
and the new dew
and the small
capture-soft
hand of you.

The Eagle
Alfred, Lord Tennyson

He clasps the crag with crooked hands;
Close to the sun in lonely lands,
Ring'd with the azure world, he stands.

The wrinkled sea beneath him crawls;
He watches from his mountain walls,
And like a thunderbolt he falls.

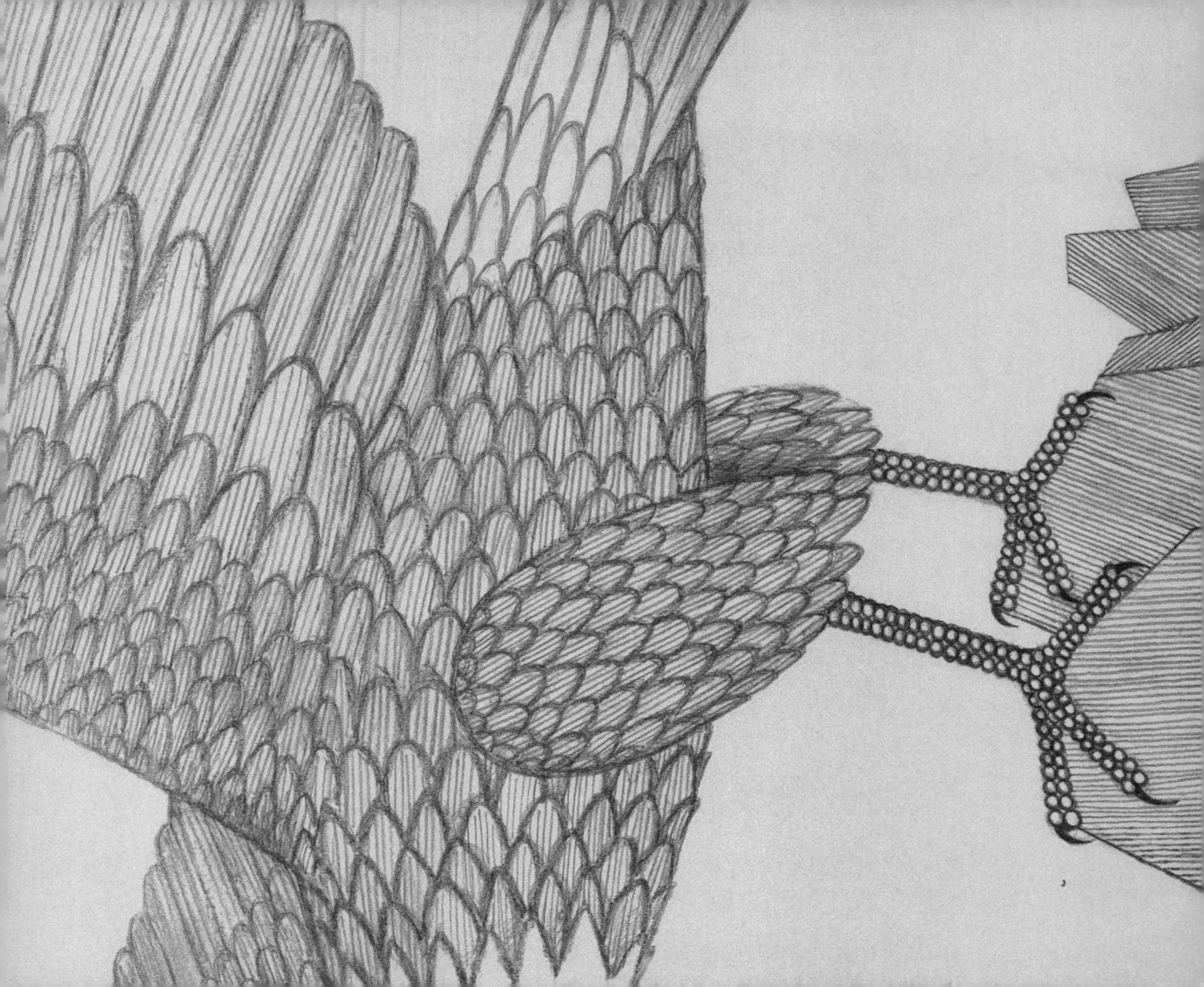

To a Squirrel at Kyle-na-no

William Butler Yeats

Come play with me;
Why should you run
Through the shaking tree
As though I'd a gun
To strike you dead?
When all I would do
Is to scratch your head
And let you go.

The Buck in the Snow

Edna St. Vincent Millay

White sky, over the hemlocks bowed with snow,
Saw you not at the beginning of evening the antlered buck and his doe
Standing in the apple-orchard? I saw them. I saw them suddenly go,
Tails up, with long leaps lovely and slow,
Over the stone wall into the wood of hemlocks bowed with snow.

Now lies he here, his wild blood scalding the snow.

How strange a thing is death, bringing to his knees, bringing
 to his antlers,
The buck in the snow.
How strange a thing—a mile away by now, it may be,
Under the heavy hemlocks that as the moments pass
Shift their loads a little, letting fall a feather of snow—
Life, looking out attentive from the eyes of the doe.

The Goat Paths

James Stephens

The crooked paths go every way
  Upon the hill—they wind about
  Through the heather in and out
Of the quiet sunniness.
And there the goats, day after day,
  Stray in sunny quietness,
  Cropping here and cropping there,
  As they pause and turn and pass,
Now a bit of heather spray,
Now a mouthful of the grass.

In the deeper sunniness,
  In the place where nothing stirs,
Quietly in quietness,
  In the quiet of the furze,
For a time they come and lie
Staring on the roving sky.
If you approach they run away,
  They leap and stare, away they bound,
  With a sudden angry sound,
To the sunny quietude;
  Crouching down where nothing stirs
  In the silence of the furze,
Crouching down again to brood
  In the sunny solitude.

If I were as wise as they
  I would stray apart and brood,
  I would beat a hidden way

Through the quiet heather spray
  To a sunny solitude;
And should you come I'd run away,
  I would make an angry sound,
  I would stare and turn and bound
To the deeper quietude,
  To the place where nothing stirs
  In the silence of the furze.
In that airy quietness
  I would think as long as they;
Through the quiet sunniness
  I would stray away to brood
By a hidden beaten way
  In a sunny solitude.

I would think until I found
  Something I can never find,
  Something lying on the ground,
  In the bottom of my mind.

The Bird of Night
Randall Jarrell

A shadow is floating through the moonlight.
Its wings don't make a sound.
Its claws are long, its beak is bright.
Its eyes try all the corners of the night.

It calls and calls: all the air swells and heaves
And washes up and down like water.
The ear that listens to the owl believes
In death. The bat beneath the eaves,

The mouse beside the stone are still as death.
The owl's air washes them like water.
The owl goes back and forth inside the night,
And the night holds its breath.

Here She Is

Mary Britton Miller

Jungle necklaces are hung
Around her tiger throat
And on her tiger arms are slung
Bracelets black and brown;
She shows off when she lies down
All her tiger strength and grace,
You can see the tiger blaze
In her tiger eyes, her tiger face.

Zebra

Isak Dinesen

The eagle's shadow runs across the plain,
Towards the distant, nameless, air-blue mountains.
But the shadows of the round young Zebra
Sit close between their delicate hoofs all day,
 where they stand immovable,
And wait for the evening, wait to stretch out, blue,
Upon a plain, painted brick-red by the sunset,
And to wander to the water-hole.

Stopping by Woods on a Snowy Evening
Robert Frost

Whose woods these are I think I know.
His house is in the village though;
He will not see me stopping here
To watch his woods fill up with snow.

My little horse must think it queer
To stop without a farmhouse near
Between the woods and frozen lake
The darkest evening of the year.

He gives his harness bells a shake
To ask if there is some mistake.
The only other sound's the sweep
Of easy wind and downy flake.

The woods are lovely, dark and deep.
But I have promises to keep,
And miles to go before I sleep,
And miles to go before I sleep.

Velvet Shoes

Elinor Wylie

Let us walk in the white snow
    In a soundless space;
With footsteps quiet and slow,
    At a tranquil pace,
    Under veils of white lace.

I shall go shod in silk,
    And you in wool,
White as a white cow's milk,
    More beautiful
    Than the breast of a gull.

We shall walk through the still town
    In a windless peace;
We shall step upon white down,
    Upon silver fleece,
    Upon softer than these.

We shall walk in velvet shoes:
    Wherever we go
Silence will fall like dews
    On white silence below.
    We shall walk in the snow.

The Prayer of the Little Ducks
Carmen Bernos de Gasztold

Dear God,
give us a flood of water.
Let it rain tomorrow and always.
Give us plenty of little slugs
and other luscious things to eat.
Protect all folk who quack
and everyone who knows how to swim.

    Amen

The Sandhill Crane

Mary Austin

Whenever the days are cool and clear
The sandhill crane goes walking
Across the field by the flashing weir
Slowly, solemnly stalking.
The little frogs in the tules hear
And jump for their lives when he comes near,
The minnows scuttle away in fear,
When the sandhill crane goes walking.

The field folk know if he comes that way,
Slowly, solemnly stalking,
There is danger and death in the least delay
When the sandhill crane goes walking.
The chipmunks stop in the midst of their play,
The gophers hide in their holes away
And hush, oh, hush! the field mice say,
When the sandhill crane goes walking.

The Sea Turtle and the Shark

Melvin B. Tolson

Strange but true is the story
of the sea-turtle and the shark—
the instinctive drive of the weak to survive
in the oceanic ark.

Driven,
riven
by hunger
from abyss to shoal,
sometimes the shark swallows
the sea-turtle whole.
"The sly reptilian marine
withdraws,
into the shell
of his undersea craft,

his leathery head and the rapacious claws
that can rip
a rhinoceros' hide
or strip
a crocodile to fare-thee-well;
now,
inside the shark,
the sea-turtle begins the churning seesaws
of his descent into pelagic hell;
then . . . *then*,
with ravenous jaws
that can cut sheet steel scrap,
the sea-turtle gnaws
. . . and gnaws . . . and gnaws . . .
his way in a way that appalls—
his way to freedom,
beyond the vomiting dark,
beyond the stomach walls
of the shark."

Prayer for Reptiles
Patricia Hubbell

God, keep all claw-denned alligators
Free.
Keep snake and lizard, tortoise, toad,
All creep-crawl
Tip-toe turtles
Where they stand,
Keep these;
All smile-mouthed crocodiles,
Young taut-skinned, sun-wet
Creatures of the sea,
Thin, indecisive hoppers
Of the shore,
Keep these;
All hurt, haunt, hungry
Reptiles
Wandering the marge,
All land-confused
Amphibians,
Sea-driven,
Keep these;
Keep snakes, toads, lizards,
All hop, all crawl, all climb,
Keep these,
Keep these.

The Ballad of Red Fox

Melvin Walker La Follette

Yellow sun yellow
Sun yellow sun,
When, oh, when
Will red fox run?

When the hollow horn shall sound,
When the hunter lifts his gun
And liberates the wicked hound,
Then, oh, then shall red fox run.

Yellow sun yellow
Sun yellow sun,
Where, oh, where
Will red fox run?

Through meadows hot as sulphur,
Through forests cool as clay,
Through hedges crisp as morning
And grasses limp as day.

Yellow sky yellow
Sky yellow sky,
How, oh, how
Will red fox die?

With a bullet in his belly,
A dagger in his eye,
And blood upon his red red brush
Shall red fox die.

Egrets
Judith Wright

Once as I travelled through a quiet evening,
I saw a pool, jet-black and mirror still.
Beyond, the slender paperbarks stood crowding;
each on its own white image looked its fill,
and nothing moved but thirty egrets wading—
thirty egrets in a quiet evening.

Once in a lifetime, lovely past believing,
your lucky eyes may light on such a pool.
As though for many years I had been waiting,
I watched in silence, till my heart was full
of clear dark water, and white trees unmoving,
and, whiter yet, those egrets wading.

Measure Me, Sky

Leonora Speyer

Measure me, sky!
 Tell me I reach by a song
Nearer the stars;
 I have been little so long.

Weigh me, high wind!
 What will your wild scales record?
Profit of pain,
 Joy by the weight of a word.

Horizon, reach out!
 Catch at my hands, stretch me taut,
Rim of the world:
 Widen my eyes by a thought.

Sky, be my depth,
 Wind, be my width and my height,
World, my heart's span;
 Loveliness, wings for my flight.

Little Things

James Stephens

Little things that run and quail
And die in silence and despair;

Little things that fight and fail
And fall on earth and sea and air;

All trapped and frightened little things
The mouse, the coney, hear our prayer.

As we forgive those done to us,
The lamb, the linnet, and the hare,

Forgive us all our trespasses,
Little creatures everywhere.

The wild geese returning
Through the misty sky—
Behold they look like
A letter written
In faded ink!

—*Tsumori Kunimoto*